Endangered and Threatened Animals

GALAPAGOS PENGUINS

by Molly Kolpin

Consultant:
Robert T. Mason, PhD
Professor of Zoology
Oregon State University

CAPSTONE PRESS
a capstone imprint

Snap Books are published by Capstone Press,
1710 Roe Crest Drive, North Mankato, Minnesota 56003.
www.capstonepub.com

Library of Congress Cataloging-in-Publication Data
Kolpin, Molly.
  Galapagos penguins / by Molly Kolpin.
      p. cm. — (Endangered and threatened animals)
  Includes bibliographical references and index.
  ISBN 978-1-4296-8431-6 (library binding)
  ISBN 978-1-62065-345-6 (ebook pdf)
  1. Galapagos penguin—Juvenile literature. I. Title.

  QL696.S473K65 2013
  598.47—dc23   2012009989

Editor: Brenda Haugen
Designer: Bobbie Nuytten
Media Researcher: Marcie Spence
Production Specialist: Kathy McColley

Photo Credits:
Alamy: David Hosking, 22, FLPA, 12, InterFOTO, 19, 25, Robert Harding Picture Library, Ltd., 14, Ville Palonen,
26; Corbis: Dr. Richard Roscoe/Visuals Unlimited, 18; iStockphoto: CraigRJD, 9 (top left), jmmf, cover, waggers33,
29; NOAA, 21, 23 (top); Shutterstock: Alfie Photography, 4, 8, (right), AridOcean, 6 (inset), CarolineTolsma,
design element, Crisan Rosu, design element, Ekaterina Lin, 23 (nets), eskymaks, 9 (bottom left), Jenny Leonard,
27, Kjersti Joergensen, 23 (hawk), Leksele, 8 (left and all middle), Moritz Buchty, 9 (bottom right), Rich Carey,
23 (garbage), Ryan M. Bolton, 9 (top right), Stacy Funderburke, 15, Stephan Kerkhofs, 13, Steve Cukrov, 28,
Tischenko Irina, 23 (bacteria)

Printed in the United States of America in North Mankato, Minnesota.
042012   006682CGF12

Table of Contents

Island Life

Chapter 1

By noon on the Galapagos Islands, the sun has reached its peak. The temperature has climbed to 100 degrees Fahrenheit (38 degrees Celsius). A group of Galapagos penguins searches for shade. They must escape from the scorching heat. With no cover in sight, the penguins dive into the ocean with a splash.

The penguins are safe for now. But blazing temperatures are just one of the challenges these animals face. For a Galapagos penguin, island life isn't always paradise. Survival is a constant struggle. There are now only about 1,500 Galapagos penguins left in the world.

Beating the Heat

Many people think penguins live only in cold, icy places. With their thick feathers, it's true that penguins were made to survive chilly environments. But Galapagos penguins are different from most other penguins. Galapagos penguins live in a **tropical** environment near the **equator**. They make their homes on the Galapagos Islands of Ecuador.

Surviving hot, tropical weather can be difficult for Galapagos penguins. They often hide in the shade. They also hold out their wings to let heat escape from their bodies. But the best way to stay cool is to jump in the ocean for a swim.

tropical: having to do with the hot and wet areas near the equator

equator: an imaginary line around the middle of Earth

Ocean Currents at Work

Temperatures on the Galapagos Islands can be very hot. But the surrounding ocean waters are usually quite cool. Sometimes the water temperature is just 60°F (16°C). Two ocean currents cause this cool water. The Cromwell Current brings cold water up from the ocean's depths. The Humboldt Current brings cold water from Antarctica to the tropical waters. Both currents also bring the fish and other ocean animals that Galapagos penguins eat.

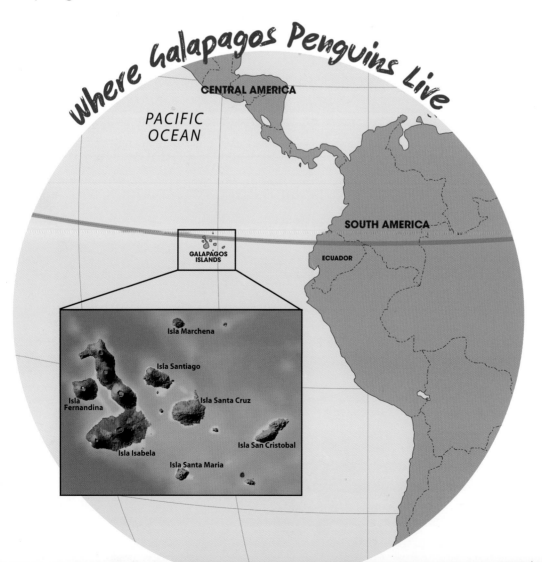

Where Galapagos Penguins Live

CENTRAL AMERICA

PACIFIC OCEAN

SOUTH AMERICA

GALAPAGOS ISLANDS

ECUADOR

Isla Marchena

Isla Santiago

Isla Fernandina

Isla Santa Cruz

Isla San Cristobal

Isla Isabela

Isla Santa Maria

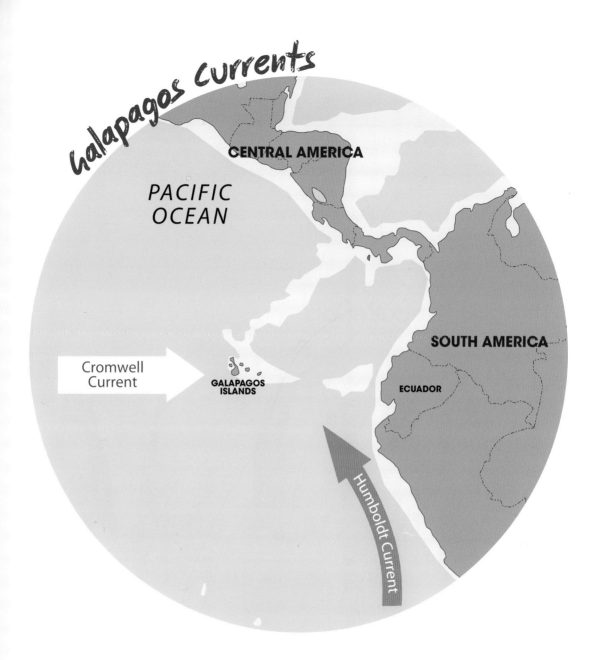

Galapagos Currents

CENTRAL AMERICA

PACIFIC OCEAN

Cromwell Current

GALAPAGOS ISLANDS

SOUTH AMERICA

ECUADOR

Humboldt Current

Without the two currents, Galapagos penguins would have trouble surviving. But sometimes the currents are changed. About every five years, an El Niño event occurs when warm waters from the west head toward the islands. When this happens, the water becomes unusually warm and kills the penguins' food sources. The penguins may starve as a result.

Galapagos penguins also face other threats, such as **predators** and pollution. The rarest penguins in the world, Galapagos penguins are considered **endangered**. They are at risk of dying out if nothing is done to save them.

Penguin Population

predator: an animal that hunts other animals for food

endangered: at risk of dying out

Unique Animals

The Galapagos Islands are located in the Pacific Ocean. The islands lie 625 miles (1,006 kilometers) west of Ecuador. These isolated, volcanic islands and the water around them are home to nearly 9,000 kinds of animals. Many of these animals can't be found anywhere else in the world. These unique animals include:

Galapagos finches

giant tortoises

marine iguanas

fur sea lions

Chapter 2

Birds of a Feather

Penguins didn't always live on the Galapagos Islands. They were most likely carried to the islands by the Humboldt Current. Over many generations, the penguins on the islands have **adapted**. They had to change in order to survive the islands' warm temperatures. Now the Galapagos penguins are their own **species**.

Physical Features

Like many other penguins, Galapagos penguins have black and white feathers. They can be identified by a thin, white band running from their eyes to below their chins. These penguins also have a black, upside-down horseshoe mark located on their stomachs.

One major difference between Galapagos penguins and other types of penguins is the length of their feathers. Galapagos penguins have shorter feathers than most other penguins. Shorter feathers help keep the Galapagos penguins from overheating.

Galapagos penguins are smaller than most other penguins. An adult Galapagos penguin stands just 16 to 18 inches (41 to 46 centimeters) tall. It weighs only about 5 pounds (2.3 kilograms). The Galapagos penguin's small size is another important change. Some penguins have extra body weight to hold in heat. But a Galapagos penguin's small frame allows heat to escape its body so it can stay cool.

adapt: to change in order to survive

species: a group of animals or plants that share common characteristics

Camouflage

Ever wonder why penguins have black and white feathers? It's because the colors act as **camouflage**. When in the water, penguins' coloring makes it difficult for predators to spot them. Viewed from below, penguins' white bellies blend in with the sky. Seen from above, their black backs blend in with the water.

Life in the Colony

Galapagos penguins are social birds. They live in **colonies** of up to 20 adult pairs. As a group, these penguins have a better chance of survival. They help one another hunt and search for food.

Galapagos penguins often go on group dives. They swim through the water at speeds up to 22 miles (35 kilometers) per hour. They catch small fish with their beaks. Sardines and mullets make up most of the penguins' diet.

Crustaceans are another important part of the penguin's diet. Many crustaceans live in the cool water around the islands. Penguins go on shallow dives to catch these small creatures. But during years when the currents change and the water becomes warm, these small animals can't survive. Then penguins have a hard time finding food.

The fringelip mullet is one of 80 different kinds of mullets found in the world. These fish are part of a penguin's diet.

camouflage: coloring or covering that makes animals, people, and objects look like their surroundings

colony: a large group of animals that live together in the same area

crustacean: a sea animal with an outer skeleton, such as a crab, lobster, or shrimp

Sounding the Alarm

Living as a group doesn't just help Galapagos penguins hunt and find food. It also means they can warn one another of approaching predators. Because they are great swimmers, penguins have few predators in the water. Sharks and seals are their main threats. But on land, the penguins have many enemies. Threats include snakes, owls, and hawks. People have also introduced predators to the Galapagos Islands, such as dogs, cats, pigs, and rats.

A penguin dives in search of food.

The Galapagos owl hunts penguins.

Galapagos penguins use calls to alert one another if a predator is nearby. Some say the calls sound like the braying noises a donkey makes. When a predator approaches, the penguins turn their backs to the predator. Their feathers blend in with the black rocks found on the islands. But this trick isn't always enough to keep them safe. Predators still kill many penguins. Animals, such as dogs and rats, sometimes destroy nests and carry diseases that harm penguins.

Chapter 3

Boosting the Population

Galapagos penguins might be endangered, but one important adaptation helps them survive. Most penguins have only one **breeding** season each year. Galapagos penguins breed all year round. They lay eggs up to three times per year.

The penguins adapted to year-round breeding because finding food around the islands is sometimes difficult. Without a steady food supply, chicks cannot survive. Galapagos penguins solve this problem by having chicks only when food is plentiful.

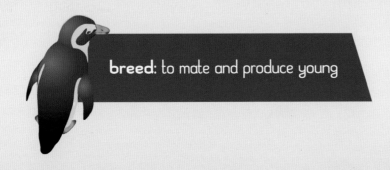

breed: to mate and produce young

Preparing for Chicks

Galapagos penguins mate for life. Females mate for the first time when they are between 3 and 5 years old. Males first mate between the ages of 4 and 6. The male and female work together to build nests for their eggs. They choose their nest sites carefully. Shade is important because too much heat and sunlight can damage eggs. Many penguins make their nests in burrows under dry lava and volcanic rock or in caves. Once a nest site is chosen, the penguins line the nest with feathers, leaves, and twigs.

Galapagos penguins often place their nests in clusters. They stay close to the nests of other penguins in their colony. Penguins work together to watch for predators that might try to steal the eggs. If predators such as snakes or crabs approach, the penguins peck at them with their beaks.

Bringing Up Baby

After Galapagos penguins mate, the female lays one or two eggs. Chicks don't hatch for another five to six weeks. During this time, parents take turns guarding the nest. Once the chicks hatch, parents care for their chicks together. Parents spit up food from their stomachs into their chicks' mouths.

Chicks are ready to live on their own once they are three to four months old.

Survival of the Fittest

Galapagos penguins often lay two eggs, but parents usually feed only the stronger chick. This way parents make sure at least one chick survives.

Two months after hatching, the chicks **molt** and grow adult feathers. These feathers protect the animals from the sun. Less than two months later, the chicks are ready to leave their parents and take care of themselves.

Galapagos penguins molting and preening

molt: shedding fur, feathers, or an outer layer of skin

19

Chapter 4

Trouble in Paradise

Galapagos penguins can live for 20 years. But few reach this age. These penguins face many dangers that make survival a struggle.

Environmental Hazards

The biggest challenge facing Galapagos penguins are El Niño events. El Niño events happen about every five years. They can last from nine months to two years. These events cause warm water from the central Pacific Ocean to replace the normally cool water around the islands. During a severe El Niño event, the water can reach 80 °F (27 °C). Such warm waters make it hard for Galapagos penguins to stay cool. The fish and crustaceans the penguins eat can't survive high water temperatures. Without these food sources, many penguins die of starvation.

The Effects of El Niño

In 1971 about 4,000 Galapagos penguins lived on the islands. But 11 years later, an El Niño event killed 77 percent of the penguins. The population had just begun to grow when a second El Niño event began in 1997. The penguin population dropped another 65 percent. Penguin numbers grow slowly. In recent years, scientists estimate that there are only about 1,500 Galapagos penguins left.

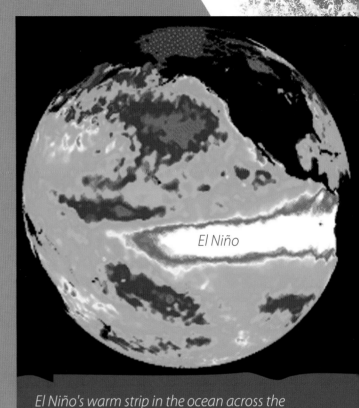

El Niño

El Niño's warm strip in the ocean across the equator in 1997

The penguins also face other natural dangers such as predators and volcanoes. Many predators live in the area. And volcanic activity is common on the Galapagos Islands. During a volcanic eruption in 1979, lava flowed into the sea. The hot lava caused the water temperature to rise. Just like during an El Niño event, the unusually warm water caused hardships for the penguins.

Human Threats

Galapagos penguins also deal with dangers caused by people and their pets. Pet cats, dogs, rats, and pigs roam freely and attack penguins' nests or young chicks. People also introduced mosquitoes to the islands. Mosquitoes carry diseases that are harmful to the penguins.

Another threat to the penguins is the growing human population. In 1970 only 4,000 people lived on the Galapagos Islands. Now the islands are home to more than 24,000 people. For the penguins, more people mean more problems.

People visiting Galapagos Islands beaches can hurt penguins in many ways.

Threats to the Galapagos Penguin

- EL NIÑO EVENTS
- NATURAL PREDATORS
- FISHING NETS
- HARMFUL GARBAGE
- DISEASE

More houses mean that penguins lose land for their nests. Garbage is another threat. Residents and tourists often throw away items that later tangle and trap the penguins. People who fish are also causing harm. Many anglers use nets to catch fish in the islands' waters. But sometimes penguins get caught in these nets and drown. People are often unaware of how their behavior affects the penguins.

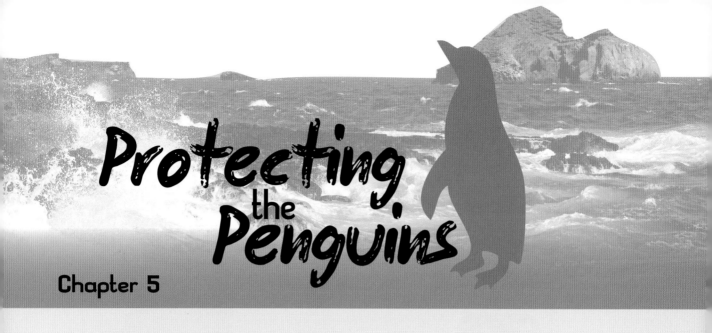

Protecting the Penguins

Chapter 5

As people become more aware of the problem, more are helping with penguin **conservation** efforts.

Galapagos Conservation Trust

The Galapagos Conservation Trust protects Galapagos Islands animals. The organization has pushed for increased protection of the 21 threatened animal species on the islands, including penguins. Now all Galapagos penguins live within the Galapagos National Park and Marine Reserve. Scientists continue watching the penguins' population. They also work to control the spread of introduced predators.

conservation: the protection of animals and plants, as well as the wise use of what we get from nature

A colony of Galapagos penguins on one of the islands' bays

Homes for Galapagos Penguins

In September 2010, researchers traveled to the Galapagos Islands to build nests for penguins. The team was led by University of Washington researcher Dee Boersma. During their time on the islands the team built 120 nests. They made nests in areas where there were no introduced predators. They also built many of the nests in groups. These groups allow the penguins to stay close together and warn one another of danger. The researchers hope the new nests will help boost the Galapagos penguin population.

Scientists are trying to increase penguin populations like the one here between Isabela and Las Tintoreas islands in Galapagos, Ecuador.

A penguin rests on the volcanic rock of the islands.

What You Can Do to Help

Do you want to help Galapagos penguins? One of the best things you can do is learn more about the animals. Then share what you learn with your family, friends, and classmates.

Another way to help Galapagos penguins is by doing your part to protect the environment. Though El Niño events occur naturally, some fear global warming may cause more frequent El Niño events in the future. People can slow global warming simply by using less energy. Turn off the lights when you leave a room. Unplug electronics when you're not using them.

27

You can also adopt a penguin through the World Animal Foundation. For a donation, you get a photo of your penguin along with an adoption certificate. You'll know you've made a difference in the lives of these struggling animals. Your money will be used to save penguin habitat and raise awareness of their problems.

Without help the Galapagos penguins will likely become extinct. By working together, people can help save these amazing birds.

Penguins on the Internet

Many groups have Web sites where you can learn more about Galapagos penguins. The following also have information about how you can help with conservation efforts.

* World Animal Foundation

* SeaWorld and Busch Gardens Conservation Fund

* Galapagos Conservation Trust

More Ways to Help

Get others involved in your mission to protect Galapagos penguins. Try the following ideas to get started.

- Learn as much as you can about Galapagos penguins. Then spread the word to others. Ask your teacher if you can do a class report on Galapagos penguins and how people can help them.

- Get some of your friends to help you with a Galapagos penguin fund-raiser. Donate the money you raise to an organization such as the SeaWorld & Busch Gardens Conservation Fund. This group raises awareness about endangered animals. It also protects animals and their habitats.

Protecting Galapagos penguin habitat will help the animals survive.

Glossary

adapt (uh-DAPT)—to change in order to survive

breed (BREED)—to mate and produce young

camouflage (KA-muh-flahzh)—coloring or covering that makes animals, people, and objects look like their surroundings

colony (KAH-luh-nee)—a large group of animals that live together in the same area

conservation (kon-sur-VAY-shuhn)—the protection of animals and plants, as well as the wise use of what we get from nature

crustacean (kruh-STAY-shuhn)—a sea animal with an outer skeleton, such as a crab, lobster, or shrimp

endangered (in-DAYN-juhrd)—at risk of dying out

equator (i-KWAY-tur)—an imaginary line around the middle of Earth; it divides the northern and southern hemispheres

molt (MOHLT)—shedding fur, feathers, or an outer layer of skin; after molting, a new covering grows

predator (PRED-uh-tur)—an animal that hunts other animals for food

species (SPEE-sheez)—a group of animals or plants that share common characteristics

tropical (TRAH-pi-kuhl)—having to do with the hot and wet areas near the equator

Read More

Ganeri, Anita. *The World's Most Amazing Islands*. Landform Top Tens. Chicago: Raintree, 2009.

Henzel, Cynthia Kennedy. *Galapagos Islands*. Troubled Treasures: World Heritage Sites. Edina, Minn.: ABDO Pub. Co., 2011.

Kalman, Bobbie, and Robin Johnson. *Endangered Penguins*. Earth's Endangered Animals. New York: Crabtree Pub. Co., 2007.

Momatiuk, Yva, and John Eastcott. *Face to Face with Penguins*. Face to Face with Animals. Washington, D.C.: National Geographic, 2009.

Internet Sites

FactHound offers a safe, fun way to find Internet sites related to this book. All of the sites on FactHound have been researched by our staff.

Here's all you do:

Visit *www.facthound.com*

Type in this code: 9781429684316

Super-cool stuff!

Check out projects, games and lots more at
www.capstonekids.com

Index